Savannah Travel Guide

Sightseeing, Hotel, Restaurant & Shopping Highlights

Gregory Bond

Copyright © 2015, Astute Press
All Rights Reserved.

No part of this publication may be reproduced, stored in a retrieval system, or transmitted, in any form or by any means without the prior written permission of the publisher, nor be otherwise circulated in any form of binding or cover other than that in which it is published and without similar condition being imposed on the subsequent purchaser.

If there are any errors or omissions in copyright acknowledgements the publisher will be pleased to insert the appropriate acknowledgement in any subsequent printing of this publication.

Although we have taken all reasonable care in researching this book we make no warranty about the accuracy or completeness of its content and disclaim all liability arising from its use

Table of Contents

Savannah **6**
    Culture **8**
    Location & Orientation **9**
    Climate & When to Visit **10**

Sightseeing Highlights **11**
    Public Squares **11**
    Forsythe Park **13**
    Juliette Gordon Low House **14**
    River Street & the Cotton Exchange **15**
    Tybee Island **17**
        Tybee Island Lighthouse 18
        Tybee Island Marine Science Center 19
    Blackbeard's Island **20**
    Old Fort Jackson **21**
    Graveyards in Savannah **22**
        Colonial Park Cemetery 22
        Bonaventure Cemetery 22
        Laurel Grove Cemetery North and South 23
    Olde Pink House **23**
    Mercer-Williams House Museum **24**
    Owens-Thomas House **24**
    Pin Point Heritage Museum **25**
    Ships of the Sea Maritime Museum **26**
    Telfair Academy **26**
    Oatland Island Wildlife Center **27**
    Cathedral of St. John the Baptist **28**
    First African Baptist Church **28**
    First Bryan Baptist Church **28**
    Independent Presbyterian Church **29**
    Christ Church **30**

Recommendations for the Budget Traveler **31**
    Places to Stay **31**
        Quality Inn Midtown 31
        Thunderbird Inn 32
        La Quinta Inn 32

    Inn at Mulberry Grove 33
    Relax Inn 33
Places to Eat 34
    Zunzi's Take Out 34
    Wiley's Championship BBQ 34
    Soho South Cafe 35
    Maxwell's 36
    The Pirates' House 36
Places to Shop 37
    River Street 37
    Fabulous Finds Under 20 37
    Fine Things Under $20 37
    Savannah Accents 38
    Go Fish Savannah 39
    The Village Craftmen 39
    River Street Market Place 40
    Shopping on Tybee Island 40
    Salt 40
    Shipwreck Jewels 40
    Latitude 32 41
    Seaside Sisters 41

Savannah

Beautiful, friendly and full of history, the city of Savannah, Georgia is famous for its role in the American Civil War. One of Savannah's squares formed the backdrop to the movie *Forest Gump* and its scenery and colorful cast of eccentrics liven the passages of the book *Midnight at the Garden of Good and Evil* by John Berendt.

The author John Berendt lived in the city for eight years whilst researching his book, which was based on a local murder, and its publication contributed to a tourist boom. A movie based on the book was also filmed here.

Other notable productions filmed in Savannah include the television mini-series *Roots* and the original *Cape Fear* movie.

From the earliest days of Savannah, General James Edward Oglethorpe, its founder had a specific and detailed vision as to the city's layout, and successive generations have continued to implement his ideals. The famous public squares have been a part of this concept from the outset and they are lovingly maintained and enjoyed by all.

The city showcases several examples of Colonial architecture and includes several landmarks from the Civil War, as well as its earlier history, glimpsed through the distinctive cover of oaks, palms and Spanish moss.

Savannah is proud of its buildings and their surroundings in the Historic District. It hosts an annual home and garden tour, every March. The English architect William Jay, who came to Savannah from his native Bath whilst in his twenties, created several of the city's distinctive facades.

For the visitor, there are various specifically themed tours to undertake through the city. Movie tours take you on an itinerary of different settings used in the production of Hollywood films, while ghost tours, whether on foot or on wheels, allow you the thrill of visiting several locations said to be haunted. With a history as rich as that of Savannah, a few lingering ghostly presences can be expected. Other tourist options focus on food, Civil War history or the appreciation of the Martini cocktail.

Culture

Savannah has a population of 136,000, of which roughly 55 percent are African-American. Caucasians compose 38 percent of the demographics, followed by Asians and Native Americans.

The people of Savannah are proud of their history. Ghosts and pirates are regularly used as themes. The Georgia Historical Society, founded in 1839, plays an active role in the preservation of heritage buildings and traditions. Its archives include the architectural details of many of its buildings, making it a valuable resource in restoration work.

Another attractive feature of Savannah is the legendary Southern hospitality. The people are friendly and hospitable. The food portions served at many eateries are generous and feature the typical flavors of Southern cooking.

The Johnny Mercer theatre, named after one of the city's more famous citizens, has hosted a variety of entertainment options, including comedy, ballet and Broadway musicals. On a more informal basis, live music and fun traditions also feature in parks, along the leisurely Waterfront region around River Street or amidst the laidback beach culture of Tybee Island.

Location & Orientation

Savannah occupies an important position as primary port along the Savannah River. It also connects to the Intracoastal Waterway, a water route that spans 4,800km along the Eastern seaboard of the United States, passing through both the Atlantic and Gulf Coasts.

Savannah is serviced by an international airport. A daily schedule links the city by direct flight to locations such as Atlanta, Dallas, New York, Washington D.C., Miami, Chicago, Detroit, Houston and Fort Lauderdale. By road it can be reached via the North-South Interstate 95 (I-95) which stretched from Maine to Florida. The Amtrak rail system connects Savannah to both Miami and New York, via the Silver Meteor and the Silver Star. The Greyhound bus network also travels to Savannah from various locations.

Once in Savannah, there are a number of options for getting around the city and its surroundings. For a tour of the Historical District, which takes an important place in the itinerary of most, you could opt for a trolley tour, which would usually allow you to hop on or off at various stops along the route. Another atmospheric mode of travel for sight-seeing is by horse drawn carriage.

Two shuttle services, the Dot and the Cat, connect various locations around the city. Both are free of charge. Other modes of transport are the River Street streetcar and the Savannah Belles Ferry system.

Climate & When to Visit

The city of Savannah falls within a sub-tropical region. It is humid throughout the year, but during the month of August, this may reach uncomfortable proportions. Rain occurs frequently, even in the summer months, when it often takes the form of thunderstorms or light showers. In the winter, rain also occurs, usually as light or moderate showers. Snowfall is extremely rare.

The city's location near the Atlantic Ocean ensures moderate temperatures throughout the year, but also places it at risk during the hurricane season between June and November.

July is generally taken to be the warmest month, with maximum temperatures averaging around 33 degrees Celsius, although a record high of 41 degrees was recorded in the mid-1980s. Even in January, the coldest month, the average high remains around 15 degrees Celsius, with the average low falling to 3.9 degrees Celsius. During the spring and autumn months, the average temperature remains in the twenties, making this an ideal time to visit, if you wish to avoid the crowds of mid-summer.

Sightseeing Highlights

Public Squares

Savannah has some charming little public squares. One of these, Chippewa Square, is well known for being the location where the movie Forest Gump was filmed.

The famous bench itself is now in the Savannah Historical Museum, but Chippewa Square also includes a statue of James Edward Oglethorpe, who initiated the original layout of Savannah, squares included. You can find Chippewa Square along Bull street, between Perry and Hull street.

Each square is located within a ward, or block of buildings. The squares vary in size. The south-north dimensions are standard at about 60m, but from east to west, they can be as wide as 91m or as narrow as 30m. They are generally marked by tall oak trees, convenient benches and wide sidewalks.

Some of the squares have particular features such as monuments, gazebos, fountains or sports facilities. They are bordered by historical buildings and often form the backdrop of celebrations, commemorations, parades or weddings.

The fountain on Lafayette Square was added to celebrate the state of Georgia's 250th anniversary and famously spouts green water on St Patrick's day. Crawford Square has a play area, basketball facilities and an attractive gazebo. In Savannah's segregated past, it was the only square African-Americans were allowed to use.

One of the newer statues, on Ellis Square, is that of the Broadway composer Johnny Mercer, also a native of Savannah. Monterey Square is another part of Savannah that features prominently in recent popular culture. It provides a central backdrop to the key setting of the book 'Midnight in the Garden of Good and Evil', by John Berendt.

The best seller focuses on the real life murder trial of Jim Williams, who lived in a mansion just off the square. A movie based on the book was shot here. Many tourists have been drawn to the city through the popularity of the book, which portrays the characteristics of the city itself as vividly as the characters of the tragic events it describes.

The original layout of Savannah, which dates back to 1733, allocated space for the first four squares, Johnson Square, Wright Square, Telfair Square and Ellis Square. James Oglethorpe, the founder of Georgia named the first and largest square after Robert Johnson, who was the governor of South Carolina at the time.

Unique to this square is the monument for Revolutionary hero Nathanael Greene. Although another square, designated in 1799, was named after Greene, his mortal remains were buried on Johnson Square. Other features include two decorative fountains, a sundial and, from 1911, the Johnson Square Business Center, Savannah's first tall building of note.

Although James Oglethorpe, the architect of Savannah's founding vision has been dead for more than 200 years, his ideals endure and are continually expanded on.

Forsythe Park

Forsythe Park comprises ten acres of land donated by William Hodgson in the 1840s and 20 more acres allocated by governor John Forsythe in the 1850s. At its heart, the Confederate Memorial can be found. The cast iron fountain at the northern side was created in 1858 and styled after a similar structure in Paris at the Place de la Concorde. It now boasts facilities for sports, paths for cycling and a fragrant garden for the vision impaired. There is also a play area for children. The periodically hosts live music or other celebratory events. It is located between Gaston Street and Park Avenue.

Juliette Gordon Low House

10 E. Oglethorpe Avenue, Savannah, GA 31401
Tel: 912 233-4501
http://www.juliettegordonlowbirthplace.org

One building that draws large numbers of pilgrims from all over America and around the world to Savannah, is the birthplace of Juliette Gordon Low, the founder of the Girl Scouts movement.

As a creative woman even in her youth, she overcame a hearing disability to pioneer one of the most popular youth movements in America. The idea came through her friendship with Sir Robert Baden-Powell, who had recently initiated the Boy Scouts and Girl Guides in the United Kingdom with the help of his sister Agnes.

The next year, 1912, saw the first gathering of Girl Scouts in the United States. The first recruit had been Juliette's niece, Margaret Gordon Lawrence also known as Daisy Doots. The movement aspired to encourage thrift, resourcefulness, helpfulness and a love of nature in young girls, regardless of status.

The house, which now belongs to the Girl Scout movement, has been restored to a 1880s decor. The life of Juliette, nicknamed Daisy, is showcased and some of her artistic creations, such as drawings, paintings and sculptures can be admired. A few of her more unusual projects included ironwork and hand painted china. There are also exhibits to illustrate the role played by her family in the history of Savannah, such as photographs and correspondence.

The jewellery items include a daisy-shaped brooch from her wedding and a Thank You, brooch associated with Mrs. Woodrow Wilson, the first Presidential spouse to serve as honorary president of the movement. Interestingly the carriage house, which later became Girl Scout club rooms, was rented for a short period by the family of the well-known poet Ogden Nash.

Juliette Gordon Low House is the most frequented museum in Georgia. Specifically it draws visits from present and past Girl Scouts of all ages.

River Street & the Cotton Exchange

River Street, which runs parallel to the Savannah River, has become a popular walk for visitors to the city of Savannah. Along the cobblestone road, it features a number of shops worth investigating, restaurants to relax in and also a great selection of city night spots.

Various interesting monuments and historical buildings punctuate its meandering length.

The Oglethorpe Bench Monument literally marks the spot where James Oglethorpe, the founder of the state of Georgia set up camp on the first night of its sojourn. The granite bench with its mosaic detail dates back to 1906 and can be viewed on Yamacraw Bluff, between Whitaker and Bay Street.

The famous Waving Girl Statue on River Street commemorates Florence Martus, the daughter of a sergeant at Fort Pulaski. Taking it upon herself to wave a handkerchief by day and a lantern by night at all passing ships from nearby Elba Island, this energetic lady soon became a legend and an institution. Although Florence died in 1942, a statue sculpted by Felix de Weldon now stands in Morrell Park to continue her self-appointed vigil.

The Old City Exchange Bell dates back to 1802. Set in an imitation steeple, it was used to call citizens to public events and meetings.

Between Bull and Broughton Street, the Georgia Hussars monument can be viewed. This elite military group was first formed by James Oglethorpe to protect the colony from hostile attack in 1742. Although it remains active, and has served the American nation in numerous conflicts, it no longer functions as a cavalry unit.

A more recent monument from 1996 commemorates the yachting races of the Atlanta Olympic Games, which were held in Savannah. At Rousakis Waterfront Plaza, stands the African American Monument, erected in 2002, with an inscription by Maya Angelou.

By virtue of its strategic location, Savannah came to play an important role in the cotton industry, not only through its own plantations, but more importantly as a base for export operations.

With the imposing figure of a winged terracotta lion presiding over the ornamental fountain at Bay and Drayton streets, the Cotton Exchange building was conceived by the architect Williams Gibbons Preston and completed in 1887. It functioned as the place where cotton prices were determined. Until the Civil War, cotton had been Savannah's most important export crop, accounting for 80 percent of its agricultural produce. One of its impressive features is the fact that it was built across Factor's Walk, an existing public street.

As a Solomon's Masonic Lodge, most of its interior is not accessible to the public. There is a popular restaurant on its premises. The Cotton Exchange can be found at 201E River Street.

Tybee Island

http://tybeeisland.com/

Located just under 29km from the city Savannah, the barrier island known as Tybee Island is a laid back haven, with a slightly eccentric coastal atmosphere, characterized by events such as kayak races, beach parties, Pirate festivals, the annual Beach Bum parade and various other art or music themed happenings.

With 8km's worth of beaches, the island offers plenty of opportunity for sunbathing or water sports. It is a popular location for surfers, as is evidenced by a number of surf shops nearby. The island also boasts plenty of opportunities to fish, from a pier or out at sea, or to observe the marshland or coastal wildlife.

Tybee City offers a number of choices for accommodation or excellent cuisine, especially seafood. In the spring and summer months, there are regular live concerts. The Tybee Island Pier and Pavilion area, along Strand Ave, provides a particularly versatile spot for entertainment, recreation or just angling.

Among the island's residents, you will find a number of talented artists and plenty of opportunities to buy their wares at galleries or craft shops.

For a spot of history, you may wish to pay a visit to the Fort Pulaski monument. Named after a Polish soldier in the Revolution, this fort was mostly abandoned as insignificant by Confederate forces. This led to its early occupation in 1863 by Union soldiers.

Tybee Island Lighthouse

30 Meddin Ave
Tybee Island
http://www.tybeelighthouse.org/

There had been at least five different towers throughout the centuries to serve the purpose of guiding naval traffic, from the earliest wooden structure ordered by General James Oglethorpe soon after the founding of Georgia, to the most recent lighthouse, which was electrified in 1933.

Several of these, including the first, were destroyed by storm. The Civil War also took its toll, as did an earthquake in 1886.

Today the lighthouse is no longer needed, but has become a popular tourist stop and backdrop for events such as weddings and music concerts. The summit of the lighthouse provides a wonderful overview of the island. The location includes a museum that provides valuable insight into the rich history of Tybee Island and a gift shop.

Tybee Island Marine Science Center

1510 Strand, Tybee Island, GA 31328Map
14th Street parking lot
Tel: 912 786 5917
http://tybeemarinescience.org

The Tybee Island Marine Science Center serves various functions with regards to both education and scientific research.

The facility features displays of sea turtles and terrapins and between May and October, when Loggerhead Sea Turtles nest and lay their eggs on the beaches of Tybee Island, groups of dedicated volunteers monitor the process and take action to protect specific clutches of eggs, if they seem to be at risk. The Center also hosts guided beach and marsh walks for $10 per adult.

A shuttle service links Tybee Island to the central part of Savannah City.

Blackbeard's Island

Pirates have played a role in various aspects of Savannah's history. Therefore it should not come as a surprise that one of the most infamous pirates of all, Edward Teach, better known as the fearsome Blackbeard once used one of the islands off Savannah as his hideout. Some legends even suggest that his treasure may still be buried somewhere on the island, although nothing has yet come to light.

Long after the time of the pirate, the Navy acquired the island as a source for timber, but from the late 1800s to early 1900s, it also served as a quarantine for sufferers of yellow fever. In1924, the island was designated a wildlife refuge.

Today Blackbeard's Island provides a sanctuary to a variety of migratory birds, and other wildlife such as storks, waterfowl, loggerhead turtles and piping plovers to name a few. The island also has deer, wild hogs and alligators. It is an excellent location for bird watching.

To protect the various resident species, certain activities are prohibited or restricted. The island is only accessible by water transport.

Old Fort Jackson

1 Fort Jackson Rd
Savannah, GA 31404
Tel: 912 232 3945
http://www.chsgeorgia.org/Old-Fort-Jackson.html

Fort Jackson is the oldest remaining fort of the state of Georgia. The fort was named after a James Jackson, a British man, who had fought in the Revolution on the American side. He later served as a governor of Georgia.

The present Fort Jackson was built in the early 1800s to replace an earlier defensive structure from the Revolutionary war. It came to good use during the Anglo-American War between 1812 and 1815, since early in 1812, American vessels had to ward off attacks from British privateers.

During the Civil War, it was controlled by the Confederate Army until December 1964, when it was surrendered to the Union forces under General William T. Sherman.

In the late 1800s, the structure was briefly known as Fort Oglethorpe. Managed by the Coastal Heritage Society, the facility now includes various educational displays and demonstrations.

Via the Islands Expressway, it is connected to the City of Savannah, Fort Pulaski and Tybee Island. Entrance is $6.

Graveyards in Savannah

Colonial Park Cemetery

Ghost tours are a popular activity amongst visitors to Savannah and one regular stop is the Colonial Park Cemetery, rumored to be haunted by several lingering ghostly presences.

One notorious legend focuses on the monstrous Rene Asche Rondolier, an 18th century murderer whose crimes were said to continue after he was executed and buried in the Colonial Park Cemetery.

The vicinity of the cemetery frequently provided settings for illegal duels, no doubt another source for unquiet spirits. As the earliest burial grounds, it still includes the graves of several pioneering residents of Savannah.

Bonaventure Cemetery

330 Bonaventure Road
Tel: 912 897-3313

Made famous by its celebrated mention in the book 'Midnight in the Garden of Good and Evil', Bonaventure Cemetery is a stop on the itenerary of many visitors to Savannah. It features a number of unusual gravestones, such as a piano shaped stone and also the singer-songwriter Johnny Mercer's bench shaped monument.

Other famous personalities buried here include Noble Wimberly Jones and Edward Telfair, two founding fathers, several Civil War generals and the poet Conrad Aiken.

Laurel Grove Cemetery North and South

More than a thousand Confederate casualties lie buried in Laurel Grove Cemetery , which is bisected by the Highway 204 into a northern and southern section. The division is not merely arbitrary. The southern section of the Laurel Grove Cemetery, which can be entered at 2101 Kollach Street, is the oldest burial ground set aside for slaves and emancipated African-Americans in Savannah.

Olde Pink House

23 Abercorn Street
Tel: 912-232-4286

If you wish to observe the twin passions of food and ghost hunting within the same location, Olde Pink House combines the two, with a dash of history thrown in. The pink stucco building, was completed in 1789 for the Habersham Family, a clan that was to be tragically divided between conflicting causes during the American Revolution.

Now a restaurant and a tavern, it is said that several of the Habershams, most notably James Habersham Jr, have appeared to employees and patrons, toasting their health or re-lighting candles at the dining tables.

Mercer-Williams House Museum

429 Bull Street
Tel: (912) 236-6352
http://www.mercerhouse.com

Mercer-Williams House is a key setting of the book 'Midnight in the Garden of Good and Evil', since the murder that is central to the events described in the book, took place here. It is located near Monterey Square.

Designed by John S Norris for General Hugh W. Mercer, it was not completed until several years after the Civil War, when John Wilder took possession of it. In the 1960s, after several years in a dilapidated state, Jim Williams bought and restored the house.

After Williams was found guilty of the murder of Danny Hansford, his sister Dorethy took ownership of it and turned it into a museum that sees a large amount of visitors each year. General Hugh W. Mercer, the original owner, was the great grandfather of the songwriter Johnny Mercer.

Owens-Thomas House

124 Abercorn Street

The house, which was finished in 1819, has been a house museum under the curatorship of the Telfair museum for more than a hundred years. It showcases several features of the English Regency style of architecture, as expressed by William Jay, who based it on buildings from his native city of Bath.

In 1825, the veranda saw the illustrious presence of the Marquis de Lafayette. It was later owned by the family of George Welshman Owens, a prominent citizen of Savannah. In her will, his granddaughter Margaret Thomas left the house to the Telfair Academy of Arts and Sciences. The collection features decorative art, mainly from the Regency period.

Pin Point Heritage Museum

Tel: 912-667-9176
http://www.pinpointheritagemuseum.com/

The building, located somewhat to the south of Savannah, was once the A.S. Varn & Son factory for processing seafood, but has been restored as a museum showcasing the lifestyle of a Gullah fishing village. It is open on Sundays or by appointment.

Ships of the Sea Maritime Museum

41 M.L. King Boulevard, Savannah, Georgia 31401
Tel: 912 232-1511
http://shipsofthesea.org

Scarborough House was once the property of William Scarborough, a key player in the steamboat industry of Savannah. Designed by William Jay, the building now houses the Ships of the Sea collection of the Maritime Museum. Some of the replicas displayed include the 'City of Savannah', 'The Anne', 'The Wanderer' and the 'Titanic'.

The museum garden is an opulent display of different colors that changes seasonally and can be rented for special events. The grounds also includes a weather station that served the city of Savannah from the 1870s to the 1940s. The gift shop includes books on Savannah and also maritime history. Admission is $8 per person for adults.

Telfair Academy

http://telfair.org/visit/telfair-academy/overview/

The Telfair Academy is one of the oldest museums in Savannah. The building is another work by the influential British architect William Jay, the former mansion of Alexander Telfair. His sister Mary left the home to the Georgia Historical Society.

Renovator Detlef Lienau conceived the sculpture garden. Art includes works by the American Impressionists Childe Hassam and Frederick Carl Frieseke, the realist George Luks and the sculptor Gari Melchers. Admission to this facility only is $12, but since it is affiliated to Owens-Thomas House and the Jepson Center, a multiple site ticket of $20.

The Jepson Center, first opened in 2006, boasts an extensive collection of contemporary art which includes works by pop artist Roy Lichtenstein, the painter/printmaker Frank Stella, photographer Richard Avedon, Jeff Koons, Jasper Johns and Chuck Close.

If you visit the complex around lunch time, do stop at Café Zeum for a fresh, green and wholesome snack.

Oatland Island Wildlife Center

711 Sandtown Road
Savannah, GA 31410
Tel: 912 395-1212

The Oatland Island Wildlife Center features a marked trail that will take you past a number of displays featuring deer, wolves, bison, cougar, birds of prey and a wetland aviary.

The aim is to keep the animals in natural environments and raised boardwalks are incorporated for part of the trail. Admission is $5 per adult.

Cathedral of St. John the Baptist

222 East Harris Street, Savannah, GA 31401
Tel: 912 233 4709

The beautifully Gothic structure of the Church of St John the Baptist is reminiscent of some of the historical churches found in Central Europe.

The oldest Roman Catholic church in Georgia, its original features have been wonderfully preserved despite a fire that nearly ravished it in 1898. The stained glass windows are the work of Inssbruck Glassmakers. It is located near Lafayette Square.

First African Baptist Church

23 Montgomery St., Savannah, GA
Tel: 912 233 6597

First Bryan Baptist Church

575 W. Bryan Street
Historic Yamacraw Village

Combined with the First Bryan Baptist Church, the First African Baptist Church represents the oldest congregation of African-American worshippers in the United States.

The church is associated with George Liele, a slave who later became an ordained minister and missionary to Jamaica. During the Civil War, the building provided sanctuary for runaway slaves and much later in the 1960s, it played a role in mobilizing African-Americans in participating in the Civil Rights Movement.

The First Bryan Baptist Church was named after Andrew Bryan, the slave who organized the congregation, and became its pastor after buying his own freedom. The building, was erected on land obtained from the Yamacraw in 1795.

The church features a beautiful stained glass window depicting the early history of African-American worship in Savannah. A monument honors George Liele, who had been Andrew Bryan's mentor. A historical plaque for Andrew Bryan, dating back to 1979, has the distinction of being the first historical landmark in Savannah to honor a black man.

Independent Presbyterian Church

25 West Oglethorpe Avenue
Tel: 912 236-3346

Designed by John Holden Greene, the graceful Independent Presbyterian Church serves a congregation that dates back to 1755. Its organist had once been the well-known hymn writer Lowell Mason. Located off Chippewa Square, it features prominently in the opening sequence of Forest Gump.

Christ Church

28 Bull Street

This church occupies the tract of land originally set aside by James Oglethorpe for the city's first church. The current building, designed by James Hamilton Couper, is in the Greek Revival style. Three prior churches had preceded it.

Two famous hymn writers, the 18th century founder of the Methodist movement, John Wesley and more recently, Francis Bland Tucker, served here. A monument to John Wesley occupies Reynolds Square, which is located near the Wesley Monumental Church.

Recommendations for the Budget Traveler

Places to Stay

Quality Inn Midtown

7100 Abercorn St., Savannah, GA 31406
Phone: (912) 352-7100
http://www.qualityinn.com/hotel-savannah-georgia-GA809

The Quality Inn Midtown is located within easy reach of the famed historic district of Savannah.

For guests, the hotel offers the use of an exercise room, a landscaped garden, an outside pool with sundeck and access to daily periodicals. Breakfast is included in the price. The dining area offers a cosy and attractive setting. Local phone calls and Internet access is free of charge. Rooms include air conditioning, coffee makers, microwaves and refrigeration. Accommodation begins at $55 a night, depending on the size of the room.

Thunderbird Inn

611 West Oglethorpe Ave, Savannah, GA 31401
Tel: 866-324-2661
http://thethunderbirdinn.com/

The Thunderbird Inn boasts lively retro interiors and rooms include television, air-condition, comfortable beds and a hairdryer. The music continues the retro theme with hits from the sixties and seventies featured. The staff are described as helpful and friendly. There is a nearby shuttle service to the tourist spots. The hotel offers free Internet access and breakfast is included in the price. Accommodation begins at $89 a night. Pets are welcome.

La Quinta Inn

Midtown, 6805 Abercorn St, Savannah, GA 31405
Tel: 912-355-3004

La Quinta Inn is located within easy reach of Savannah's popular historical district.

The hotel has a large outdoor pool with a sundeck for swimming or sunbathing. Rooms have cable TV, free Internet access, a coffeemaker, hairdryer and plug-and-play data port. There are several shops and restaurants nearby. Accommodation begins at $59 a night. The price includes breakfast.

Inn at Mulberry Grove

101 O'Leary Road at I95 Exit 109
Port Wentworth, GA 31407
T: (912) 965-9666
http://www.innatmulberrygrove.com/

Inn at the Mulberry Grove is located just off Exit 109 off Intestate 95 and just a 15 minute drive away from Savannah's historical district. The decor presents an attractive first impression. Room conveniences include a coffee maker, refrigerator, flat screen TV and free Internet access. There is a beautiful garden patio. Breakfast is free and includes a large variety of options. Accommodation rates begin at $56 a night.

Relax Inn

11211 Abercorn Street, Savannah, GA 31419
Tel:-927-7777
http://www.relaxinnsavannah.com/

Located ten minutes from the historical district, there are several malls and restaurants to explore nearby.

Staff are friendly and eager to please. Rooms include television with 75 channels, refrigeration and microwave facilities, free Internet, free coffee and free local calls. Accommodation begins at $50 a night.

Places to Eat

Zunzi's Take Out

108 E York St, Savannah, GA 31401
Tel: 912 443 9555
http://zunzis.com

Zunzi's is a great location if you wish to pick up affordable food. There are a number of vegetarian choices, such as the Veggie Wrap, curries, pizza and pasta. There is also a selection of salads, burgers and sandwiches including a monster bite known as The Godfather. Expect to pay between $5 and $10 per item.

Wiley's Championship BBQ

4700 Highway 80 East, Suite N, Savannah, GA 31410
Tel: 912 201 3259
http://www.wileyschampionshipbbq.com/

Meat features prominently on the menu at Wiley's.

Portions are generous, and present good value for money. For ribs, there is a choice between beef or pork. Side items include choices such as sweet potato chips, Brunswick stew, several options with beans, including the somewhat immodestly named Best Beans on the Planet, the usual french fries, potato salad and Dutch Crust Sweet potato casserole. There are a number of dessert options, including a Bourbon chocolate pecan pie. Expect to pay between $10 and $25 for most items.

Soho South Cafe

12 W Liberty St, Savannah, GA 31401-3906
Tel: 912-233-1633
http://www.sohosouthcafe.com

Soho South Cafe is open for lunch on weekdays and brunch on Sundays. Some of the brunch menu highlights include the Southwestern Burrito, Shrimp and Grits, omelets and waffles. For lunch the choice is more extensive. There is a large variety of sandwiches, salads and desserts.

A few of the more exotic choices include Crab & Artichoke Quiche, the Waldorf-style Tuna Pita, the Cuban Panini and the Char-grilled Strube Farms Beef Burger. A number of favorites such as Andalusian Chicken Salad, Lump Crab Cakes and Chicken Pot Pie are also available for takeaway from the deli section. Nearly all items are under $15.

Maxwell's

109 Jefferson Street, Savannah, GA
Tel: 912-349-5878
http://www.maxwellssavannah.com/

Dinner at Maxwell's resembles the concept of Mediterranean dining where instead of one main dish, a number of small plates can be ordered to sample. These include items such as Buffalo Milk Mozzarella Bruschetta, Stuffed Waygu Beef, Marinated Lamb Loin Chops and Seared Sea Scallops. There is also a soup of the day and a selection of salads and desserts. The lunch menu includes a range of sandwiches, while the Sunday brunch includes a range of speciality items. Most items are priced between $8 and $18.

The Pirates' House

20 East Broad St., Savannah, GA 31401-2929
Tel: 912 233-5757
http://www.thepirateshouse.com/

For a spot of dining with a difference, why not check in at the Pirate's House. Dating back to the mid-18th century, the Pirate's House restaurant boasts plenty of history, atmosphere and even a ghostly presence or two.

Some of the house specialities include chicken gumbo, a variety of seafood baskets, Savannah Shrimp Creole, Chicken Jambalaya and Mango Chilli Glazed Salmon. For lunch, expect a variety of sandwiches and burgers, such as the Crab melt or the Slick Chick. There are also salads and soups to choose from. Most menu items are charged at under $25. The venue also hosts pirate parties

Places to Shop

River Street

Fabulous Finds Under 20

207 E. River St., Savannah, GA 31401
912-447-6666
http://www.fabulousfindsunder20.com/

Fine Things Under $20

121 W. River St., Savannah, GA 31401
Tel: 912-232-1995
http://www.finethingsundertwenty.com/

Savannah Accents

211 W. River St., Savannah, GA 31401
Tel: 912-234-3331

Not only is River Street a pleasant waterfront area to relax and stroll about, it also offers a few great shops to check out. At Fabulous Finds Under 20, you will discover great accessories such as purses, purse hooks and scarves, all priced as the name promises, under $20. With a similar theme, there is Fine Things under $20.

For snacks, do pay a visit to River Street Sweets, the city's oldest candy store, Savannah's Candy Kitchen, the largest candy store or the Peanut Shop of Savannah, which boasts the largest variety in peanut related treats.

True Grits offers Civil War or maritime themed memorabilia. Visit Savannah Accents to take a little piece of the hospitable city home with you, whether in the form of a Laura Deen cookbook, charms for your bracelets or troll beads. Book lovers should check out the stock at Books on Bay, which ranges from 18th century tomes to more recent publications.

Go Fish Savannah

106 West Broughton Street, Savannah GA 31401
Tel: 912 231-0609
http://www.shopgofish.com

Shop Go Fish is the perfect place to visit if you believe in shopping with a conscience. The mission statement of this enterprise is to purchase goods from artisans in developing nations at fair prices. Wares range from beaded jewellery, to clothing, to scarves, hairpins and handbags. Gift items include picture frames, trinket boxes, mosaic items and carved animals such as cats, birds and giraffes. Products originate from locations such as Thailand, Indonesia and Central America.

The Village Craftmen

223 West River Street, Savannah, Georgia
Tel: 912 236-7280
http://thevillagecraftsmen.com/

It is always satisfying to buy art and craft items directly from the people who produce them. A wide range of skills are represented in this craft co operation. Wares include glass objects, kitchen utensils, restored photographs from Savannah's past, decorative oyster shell art, children's smocked dresses, quilts, ornamental ironwork, pottery and paintings.

River Street Market Place

http://www.riverstreetmarketplace.com

River Street Market Place occupies a collection of sheds that, together with the cobblestoned surface, evoke an atmosphere of the 1800s. Some of the wares sold include leatherwork, jewellery, clothing such as T-shirts and hats as well as a variety of gift items.

There are also food vendors and benches that offer the opportunity to simply relax and enjoy a view of the Savannah River.

Shopping on Tybee Island

Tybee Island is home to a vibrant community of eccentrics and artisans, many of whom sell their wares on the island to visitors.

Salt

24 Tybrisa Street
Tybee Island, Georgia
Tel: 912 786-8833
http://www.saltartisan.com

Shipwreck Jewels

1601 Inlet Ave
Tybee Island, Georgia 31328

Latitude 32

1213 Highway 80, Unit M
Tybee Island, Georgia 31328
Tel: 912 786-9334
http://www.latitude32.us

Seaside Sisters

1207 Hwy 80 East
Tybee Island, Georgia 31328
Tel: 912 786-9216
www.seasidesisterstybee.com

Salt Artisan sells soap, candles and a whole range of bath and beauty products. Expect a range of casualwear for men, women and children at Lattitude 32. Gallery by the Sea features a good selection of functional and wearable art. For jewellery and other gifts, visit Shipwreck Jewels. Seaside Sisters boasts a wide range of wares, including antiques, accessories, books and art.

Printed in Great Britain
by Amazon